LITERARY ACCENTS

Literary Accents
A Literary Journal

Volume 1, Issue 1

Katerina Stoykova, Editor

Accents Publishing • Lexington, Kentucky • 2019

Copyright © 2019 by Accents Publishing
All rights reserved

Printed in the United States of America

Accents Publishing
Editor: Katerina Stoykova
Cover Image: *Hare* by Albrecht Durer, 1528

ISBN: 978-1-936628-51-3
First Edition

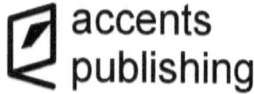

Accents Publishing is an independent press for brilliant voices. For a catalog of current and upcoming titles, please visit us on the Web at

www.accents-publishing.com

CONTENTS

From the Editor / ix

The Untied Stales / *Paul Hostovsky / 1*
Philately / *Paul Hostovsky / 2*
Existential Morning / *Vincent J. Tomeo / 4*
Fashion Statement / *Vincent J. Tomeo / 5*
In the Alley / *Kirsten Morgan / 6*
Social Workers I've Noticed / *Daniel Coshnear / 7*
Between Bad and Luck / *Dean Crawford / 8*
Me and Los Angeles / *Mark Lee Webb / 9*
Cloud Window / *Warren Woessner / 10*
After the Argument / *Amy Watkins / 11*
Nothing Good Can Come / *Marilyn Kallet / 12*
Smug / *Marilyn Kallet / 13*
Wish I Hadn't Seen That / *Marilyn Kallet / 14*
Fox Suddenly Decides / *Katharyn Howd Machan / 15*
In Sleep / *Karen George / 16*
Revenant / *Karen George / 17*
Out of Chaos / *Karen George / 18*
I'll Be There / *Mary Ann Savage / 19*
Lady's Choice, He Said / *Pauletta Hansel / 20*
Me Too / *Pauletta Hansel / 21*
The Heartbreak Tree / *Pauletta Hansel / 22*
How It Begins / *Jean Tucker / 23*
Sucker / *Christopher McCurry / 24*
Silence / *Christopher McCurry / 25*
Accusation / *Christopher McCurry / 26*

Marriage / *Tina Parker* / 27
The Day They Came for Me / *Tina Parker* / 28
Patient Interview / *Tina Parker* / 29
Burning Bed / *Hugh Findlay* / 30
Black and White Photo / *Geo. Staley* / 31
The Girl With No Eyes / *Geo. Staley* / 32
Sated / *Catherine Perkins* / 33
Fragment / *Chuck Stringer* / 34
Infinitesimal the Distance / *Carmen Germain* / 35
Exiled / *Carmen Germain* / 36
Tweet Poem / *Diane Kendig* / 37
Tweet Poem Two / *Diane Kendig* / 38
Every Solution Has a Problem / *Carol Levin* / 39
Math, at the Doctor's Office / *Marian Kaplun Shapiro* / 40
All I Know / *Bo Niles* / 41
Some Days / *Laura Clewett* / 42
Story / *Laura Clewett* / 43
Ten Forms of Silence / *Laura Clewett* / 44
Beneath / *Libby Falk Jones* / 45
Mountain Invitation / *Libby Falk Jones* / 46
You Can Always Add; You Can't ... / *Libby Falk Jones* / 47
Transportation / *Anita Wilkins* / 48
Discovery, on the Ferry to Skyros / *Anita Wilkins* / 49
Archery / *Anita Wilkins* / 50
Solstice / *Dennis J. Preston* / 51
Reunion / *Dennis J. Preston* / 52
20 Years After Paralysis / *Laverne Zabielski* / 53
Giving Up / *Bill Glose* / 54

Another Party / *Nancy LaChance* / 55
There were crossways of stars / *Margarita Serafimova* / 56
Above the Orchard / *Young Smith* / 57
Out on the Kayak / *Young Smith* / 58

Accent on Accents / 59

The Wild Raw Green of Kentucky / *Pat Williams Owen* / 60
Cervix / *Pat Williams Owen* / 61
Confirmation / *Pat Williams Owen* / 62
Pedestrians / *Pat Williams Owen* / 63
Reification / *Pat Williams Owen* / 64

The Poets / 65

About Accents and Its Senior Editor / 71

FROM THE EDITOR

Dear Friend,

Thank you for picking up this magazine. We are thrilled to share with you our very first issue. It features 56 poems of up to 50 words by 35 masters of the short poem.

We hope you enjoy every word in this issue!

To all our subscribers, contributors, readers and supporters, thank you! May reading and writing bring to you much inspiration and joy.

Sincerely,

Katerina Stoykova
Senior Editor

THE UNTIED STALES
Paul Hostovsky

of America, my daughter
has written over the map
of the lower forty-eight
a little carelessly,
transposing two letters,
forgetting to cross one *t*,
the map itself colored in
a little sloppily, dark crayon
spilling in from Canada
and bleeding into Mexico.
And how perfect is that?

PHILATELY
Paul Hostovsky

sounds
vaguely
sexual.
Like *fellatio*.
It's the *l*'s,
the liquids,
the licking
of stamps,
lovers
of stamps—
from the
Greek, *phil*,
which is love
combined
with *ateleia*,
which is
tax collection,
which isn't
very sexy.
But stamp
collectors
everywhere

took a fancy
to the word,
and it stuck.

EXISTENTIAL MORNING
Vincent J. Tomeo

Rays of light burst through the dense fog.
On a park bench,
a man wrapped in a wrinkled plastic garbage bag
keeps scratching, scratching, scratching.

The sun becomes a rainbow.

FASHION STATEMENT
Vincent J. Tomeo

December 1966.
Bitter cold.
He was afraid to go to school.
He had no money for a winter coat.
He had to borrow mama's quilt blanket.

He entered the classroom,
students stared,
said nothing.

By the end of December,
Everyone wore a blanket.

IN THE ALLEY
Kirsten Morgan

Behind the
homeless clinic

stenciled
on a dumpster

NO BABIES

SOCIAL WORKERS I'VE NOTICED
Daniel Coshnear

dress with a little flare
pantsuits, yes
and sensible shoes
but a feather in the hair
or a medallion
glued with shells
a brooch big as a brick
handmade by the kids
one flight up
in oncology

BETWEEN BAD AND LUCK
Dean Crawford

Tides of misfortune come and go,
high and low.

I test the waters with a timorous toe
looking for a place between bad
and luck to dig a hole.

ME AND LOS ANGELES
Mark Lee Webb

It's complicated.
Like we lay together
in the same bed
but don't sleep
with each other.
Because this place is really
chicken noodle,
occasional stir-fry.
Cleveland in culottes.
Des Moines wearing Tommy Bahama.
Accidental fruit fermentation
    a layered acrylic interpretation of acid rain.

CLOUD WINDOW
Warren Woessner

Blocks from here, towers
scrape the sky.
In this warehouse,
workers who scrape to get by,
strain to see the sky.
One window tipped open
catches clouds,
keeps them outside.

AFTER THE ARGUMENT
Amy Watkins

Last night the jasmine opened
a yellow profusion, pale as starlight
reaching toward the waxing moon.
This morning the blossoms
have closed like stars winking out,
like an oil lamp turned down,
its flame folding in then disappearing.
Not a hint of the fragrance lingers.

NOTHING GOOD CAN COME
Marilyn Kallet

Your wife was right.
You were dreaming
Me. You promised her
No more porn and no more
Teacher fanboy.

The sky omens agreed:
Ironic blue, no touch of you-
And-me.
The clouds have moved on.
I should, too.

SMUG
Marilyn Kallet

Writing to you, Captain, humbles,
teaches the ontology of null-
and-void. The exercise of
male privilege is a language. You'll
reply when you're bad
and ready. Now I know the etymology
of smug. Excuse me,
sir, I thought we were
friends. Didn't mean
to disturb.

WISH I HADN'T SEEN THAT
Marilyn Kallet

George the handyman slides out his teeth,
honors the chicken hot wings.
"At home, I have two ghosts, man and woman,"
he announces, digs in.
"How do you know one's a woman?" Peg asks.
"She slams doors," he says. "No man does that."

FOX SUDDENLY DECIDES
Katharyn Howd Machan

she's platinum.
She's *crème de la crème*:
perfection.
Doesn't matter she never knew
why her brother wandered.
Doesn't matter her best kit
killed herself with poison.
She's the queen, alive.
Dancing where the forest starts.
Skipping: black feet blameless.

IN SLEEP
Karen George

> ~ Found poem composed from Jane Hirshfield's
> "Of Amplitude There is No Scraping Bottom"

dark stories peel from her
a door opens into green unknowing
mountains   mushrooms
a padlocked house   diagonal windows
inside   a bear rummages
for a pearl   in a hinged nest

REVENANT

Karen George

> ~ Found poem composed of words from
> Eavan Boland's poem "What Love Intended"

Out the window
a burning poplar
a small quarrel of rain

A past love
the smell of limes
skates through a cracked door

The yellow bloom of pain
places you on a balance beam
of grace and ruin

OUT OF CHAOS
Karen George

> ~ Found poem composed/modified from words in Ada Limón's poem, "The Whale and the Waltz Inside of It"

Imagine a blue cave
at the edge of the world.

By the dizzying bliss of a fire
a woman spins suffering

into letters of the original language.
An old river, golden mother of tongues,

bears down on the land,
sings of depth and borders, crossing.

I'LL BE THERE
Mary Ann Savage

Later
at a desk called mine
or on my bed with a book,
I'll still be there
across the lake with you,
sunlight all around us
and birds we can't see
calling, calling.

LADY'S CHOICE, HE SAID
Pauletta Hansel

easy or hard, either way
he would take me, so I who'd
already took from his cheap
pink wine, took in his pink cock
too. I knew I was easy.
I knew I'd said no. I can't
tell one without the other.

ME TOO
Pauletta Hansel

Because I, too,
was once thirteen,
because I did not
k[no]w
I was too
beautiful, because
he could,
because everybody knew
this flesh was what defined me,
because men will be
boys, because I was
a perk of the job,
because
I only wanted
to be seen.

THE HEARTBREAK TREE
Pauletta Hansel

The magnolia—bud, blossom,
decay all on one gnarled branch.
In the nursing home,
my mother asks, "Do you ever
shut your eyes and wonder,
whatever happened to *me*?"

HOW IT BEGINS
Jean Tucker

A shivering bus stop.
Arm in arm for the first time.
The sky a broken-into jewelry box.

SUCKER
Christopher McCurry

So this is what not being able to stop
    thinking about you
    tastes like.

SILENCE
Christopher McCurry

has made a father
out of me.

ACCUSATION
Christopher McCurry

I'm not saying
I think there's
another man

but you have
showered

three times
in two days
and I haven't
once.

MARRIAGE
Tina Parker

I confess I felt trapped
From the first week
I fell into a malaise
Quite deep
They all talked about me
But I had no one
When the sickness came
It felt a relief.

THE DAY THEY CAME FOR ME
Tina Parker

I sliced open the sun
I walked the tight rope
And touched the moon

I drank stars that day
I danced with a tree
Climbed into thunder

The day they came for me
I cartwheeled into the sea
And sang open the snow.

PATIENT INTERVIEW
Tina Parker

Do you have visions
Hear voices
Did you drink in the darkness
See how bright it fills you?

BURNING BED
Hugh Findlay

Let us sleep
Without love tonight
Without pain

Let us arch our backs
In desire
And satisfy nothing

We two
So fragile
So beyond shame

Hurt
Turn over
Hurt again

BLACK AND WHITE PHOTO
Geo. Staley

    Mission, So. Dak.—1983

I point out the coffee mug,
my name in cursive.
My wife says,
    "I bought it for you in Ohio."

In another state,
in a voice not my wife's,
    "So ... your name's George."

THE GIRL WITH NO EYES
Geo. Staley

She asked, "What is good poetry?"
He answered her with a poem.
She asked, "Is this good poetry?"
He answered her with another poem.
She never asked again.

SATED
Catherine Perkins

I walk with my eyes,
eat with my ears,
hear with my tongue,
feel with my nose,
and see with my mouth.
No wonder I am so full.

FRAGMENT
Chuck Stringer

gleaming white in the sand,
open like a cradle, half of a
wave-tossed bivalve
still trying to catch
the sea

INFINITESIMAL THE DISTANCE
Carmen Germain

between before and after.
How a travel trailer veers
from its tow path into my lane
seeming to pass as ghost
through my windshield

before correcting.
Somewhere a man balances a ladder.
A woman leaves her home
for the last time, not knowing
it's the last time.

EXILED

Carmen Germain

How the fat moon
after weeks of cloud
skims cedar trees
unlike the Equator moon

straight up like a coin
ready to drop
a kind of luck.
Back then I strained for it,

leaning to see God
flame through Adam,
everything still possible.

TWEET POEM

Diane Kendig

Life is too brief/ for tweets/ teeny spurts of meaning/ keep swelling and bursting beyond/ this slim seam of ore./ I need more.

TWEET POEM TWO
Diane Kendig

Still: SOS, OK, lol./ Less is lots./ Whatever I'm allotted/ I'll build out or up,/ count down or go over.

EVERY SOLUTION HAS A PROBLEM

Carol Levin

Sound like beetle wings
shaking begins it. Then
a simultaneous tap dance
of drops. The coffee maker
moans; little burps
end the cycle before
one/two/three/
pitched to pierce beeps.
Morning jolted
caffeine fueled
my jaguar roar
fires-up neighbors
who call the cops.

MATH, AT THE DOCTOR'S OFFICE
Marian Kaplun Shapiro

i + ll = ill.
we + ll = well.
Nonsense to notice
while waiting
       and waiting …

ALL I KNOW
Bo Niles

loss weeps
into the desert
of an empty bed.

tears
when they come
salt the underskin
of each eyelid

the truth of tears
is precious
when heart and bed
are scoured
and all that remains
is a memory of air

I shall live on air

SOME DAYS
Laura Clewett

Every step
takes effort

every breath
is incomplete

every cell
shudders

The hours loom
like planets

undiscovered

STORY
Laura Clewett

I once knew a girl
who could read
people's minds.

Like a sponge,
she absorbed
images emotions ideas

from the atmosphere.
She did not tell
me this—somehow

I just knew.

TEN FORMS OF SILENCE
Laura Clewett

The silence of secrets.

The silence
        of omission.

The silence of fear.

The silence of after.

The silence of snow.

The silence of shadows.

The silence of darkness.

The silence of sleep.

The silence of death.

The silence of prayer.

BENEATH
Libby Falk Jones

Under brittle rock
whose jagged edge
could slice
a careless kneecap,
heat surges,
flows to blue pools
with cut-glass surfaces,
magnets for souls
and bodies
in restless search
of peace.

MOUNTAIN INVITATION
Libby Falk Jones

There's nothing much to do here—
just gather wildflowers

and blueberries, watch
clouds climb, make tea

and love, listen to rain
on the tin roof, nap

in the hammock, read
good books and write.

You say this sounds like
heaven? You're welcome.

YOU CAN ALWAYS ADD; YOU CAN'T SUBTRACT
Libby Falk Jones

My mother's maxim, handwritten
on the last page of the cookbook
she made for her only child,
going off into the world
at 22 not knowing how to season
gumbo or even scramble an egg—

but I had to let her go.

TRANSPORTATION
Anita Wilkins

The gladiolas are getting
too tall for their roots
and lean out, all together

like a crowd watching
down the street
for the bus.

DISCOVERY, ON THE FERRY TO SKYROS
Anita Wilkins

I have the touch of it now!
It's like pulling the lizard
along by its tongue

while it laughs
and lashes the sand with its tail.

That's the poem,
left there on the sand
after we've both
gone by.

ARCHERY
Anita Wilkins

The tortoise-shell cat
leaps at and misses

a moth

turns, yawns
and arches her back

so
exquisitely high that (leaping
upward toward one bright star)

the whole twilight
turns

and stretches itself in a blue arch
from rim to rim

SOLSTICE

Dennis J. Preston

falling snow, sleet and ice
affixes itself onto limbs
and lane with grace and delicacy
of an arctic hare
danger awaits on every turn
accumulation to devastation
watchful eye can't see beyond
timber wolf awaits her prey

REUNION
Dennis J. Preston

I can't believe
I had to ask

who you were,
not that

you've changed
or anything.

Me either.

20 YEARS AFTER PARALYSIS
Laverne Zabielski

I saw your determined independence.

Could you put my clothes in the dryer, please?
Empty my urine bag?
Fill my water bottle?

Cell phone tied to a string.
Car keys on the same hook.
Baseball caps on a shelf.
The stick you used to retrieve them.

GIVING UP
Bill Glose

Lent again—I suggest Sophia
give up the cancer in her lung

and she offers that wry smile
that made me fall in love.

We neither mention the coming
chest-constricted days of brittle air

nor her .38 special in its velvet bag,
the many modes of giving up.

ANOTHER PARTY
Nancy LaChance

balloons pop
tiny papers explode
meanwhile
snow swirls like confetti
another invite
to a winter party

***

Margarita Serafimova

There were crossways of stars
and a deer with a raised head.
My heart was empty, but I had trees.

ABOVE THE ORCHARD
Young Smith

Above the orchard this afternoon,
a clutch of starlings—

a dark fist
that closes and opens
in the sky.

OUT ON THE KAYAK
Young Smith

A great rock wall beside the river.
On the other side, pastureland—

low, muddy places where cattle wade.
The water is green and still.
It drips from the paddle onto my arms and lap.

Turkey vultures circle high overhead.
Dragonflies light on my knees.

ACCENT ON ACCENTS

We'd like to take this opportunity to bring to your attention one of our latest full-length books, *Orion's Belt at the End of the Drive* by Pat Williams Owen. We are very proud of Pat and her work and wanted to feature several very short poems from her book.

> Her poetry is the practice of interrogating reality in order to understand one's place in the world.
>
> —Jeremy Paden

> Pat Owen is that rare poet who witnesses the divine in actually lived lives—in wrinkles and cafés, otters and baseball, vulvas and ferns.
>
> —Rebecca Gayle Howell

> I am most struck by a sense of acceptance resonant in these poems but also the necessary, conscious practice to preserve that acceptance.
>
> —Maureen Morehead

http://www.accents-publishing.com/orionsbelt.html

THE WILD RAW GREEN OF KENTUCKY

After the tropics
there's a wild raw wind here
cutting through my shirt.
The world's so proud when it's sunny
as though anything is possible
after so much rain.
Maple limbs sway
just as they did
centuries ago
for my forbearers.

CERVIX

Numb and dumb,
like the tip of a penis,
but without the feeling.
It's always been
that warm marble
with an eye
at the top of the vaginal canal.
Now collapsed, falling out,
emerging finally
to see the world.

CONFIRMATION

All dressed up
girls in dresses and sandals
boys in dress shirts and slacks
all clean and shiny
smiling for the cameras
age 14
with their rounded shoulders
anticipation of so much weight
already there.

PEDESTRIANS

Waddling across the yard
in late afternoon shadows
heads down vigilant
a pair of female mallards.

What do they seek
squat to the ground
travelling on thin orange legs?

REIFICATION

A quick fix to the terrifying anxiety of living
in a vast dark world: we put in a box
all power and then pray to it,
never acknowledging that nothing
in the universe is separate
from anything else.
Nothing stands alone, unpermeated.

THE POETS

In order of appearance:

Paul Hostovsky's latest book of poetry is *Late for the Gratitude Meeting* (Kelsay Books, 2019). His poems have won a Pushcart Prize and two Best of the Net awards.

Vincent J. Tomeo is a poet, archivist, historian and community activist. To date, Mr. Tomeo has 837 published poems/essays; winner of 105 awards; 115 public readings.

Kirsten Morgan loves capturing life's marrow into condensed packages. A teacher of children, homeless women and seniors, she finds that extraneity often gets into the way of essence.

Daniel Coshnear works at a group home and teaches through UC Berkeley Extension. He is author of two story collections: *Jobs & Other Preoccupations* (Helicon Nine 2001), Willa Cather Award winner, and *Occupy & Other Love Stories* (Kelly's Cove Press 2012). In 2015 he won the Novella Award from Fiction Fix (now Flock) for *Homesick Redux*.

Dean Crawford is a Kentuckian. He graduated from the University of Kentucky a long time ago with a B.A. He writes poetry and fiction occasionally publishing some of it.

Mark Lee Webb received an MFA from Queens University of Charlotte. He has published two chapbooks, and his work has appeared in many literary magazines.

Warren Woessner is the co-founder and Senior Editor of *Abraxas* magazine and press. His most recent collection of poetry is *Clear All the Rest of the Way* (The Backwaters Press) and *Exit ~ Sky* (Holy Cow! Press).

Amy Watkins is the author of *Milk & Water* and the art editor for *Animal: A Beast of a Literary Magazine*. She lives in Orlando with her husband and daughter.

Marilyn Kallet is Poet Laureate of Knoxville and author of 18 books, including *How Our Bodies Learned*. Dr. Kallet is Professor Emerita at the University of Tennessee. She leads workshops for VCCA-France.

Katharyn Howd Machan, professor of Writing at Ithaca College, has published 38 poetry collections, most recently *What the Piper Promised*, winner of the 2018 New Alexandria Quarterly Press chapbook competition.

Karen George is author of the poetry collections *Swim Your Way Back* (2014) and *A Map and One Year* (2018) from Dos Madres Press. She reviews poetry at *http://readwritepoetry.blogspot.com/*.

Mary Ann Savage lives in Manassas, Virginia.

Pauletta Hansel's sixth poetry collection is *Palindrome* (Dos Madres Press), winner of the 2017 Weatherford Award. She was Cincinnati's first Poet Laureate and edits *Pine Mountain Sand & Gravel*.

Jean Tucker, of Louisville, Kentucky, has poems in many journals and in a chapbook based on experiences in Greece. When not traveling, she is thinking about it.

Christopher McCurry is a teacher and writer. He is the cofounder of Workhorse, a publishing company and community for working writers.

Tina Parker is the author of the poetry collections *Mother May I* and *Another Offering*. These poems spring from research into the lives of women labeled as "other."

Hugh Findlay lives in Durham, North Carolina, formerly of Lexington, Kentucky. His work has appeared in several literary publications, including *The Dominion Review* and *Tiny Seed Literary Journal*.

Geo. Staley is retired from teaching at Portland Community College. *Arc of the Ear*, his 3rd chapbook of poems, was released by Finishing Line Press in July 2015.

Catherine Perkins, the mother of one daughter, is a retired Thoroughbred trainer and farmer. Catherine has 6 poems published by local publishers—Accents,

Workhorse, and The Bourbon Co. Citizen. She loves to write, paint and perform stand-up comedy.

Chuck Stringer's poems have appeared in *Pine Mountain Sand & Gravel*, *The Licking River Review*, *Words*, and *For a Better World*. He lives and writes by Fowlers Fork in Union, Kentucky.

Also a visual artist, **Carmen Germain** is the author of *These Things I Will Take with Me*. Her new collection, *The Old Refusals*, has just been released from MoonPath Press and features her cover art, *Fantasia in the Key of Yellow*.

Diane Kendig's five poetry collections include *Prison Terms* (2017.) She has published prose and poetry in journals such as *J Journal*, *Under the Sun*, and *Wordgathering*. Website: *http://dianekendig.com/*.

Carol Levin is the author of three full volumes: *An Undercurrent of Jitters*, *Confident Music Would Fly Us to Paradise*, *Stunned By the Velocity*. Also two chapbooks. She's an Editorial Assistant at *Crab Creek Review*.

Marian Kaplun Shapiro, five times Senior Poet Laureate of Massachusetts, is the author of three books of poetry. She practices as a psychologist in Lexington, Massachusetts.

Bo Niles began making and publishing poems after a career writing about home design. She is a member of the 92nd Street Y's senior poetry group in New York City.

Laura Clewett is working on an MFA in Creative Nonfiction at the University of Kentucky. She has been writing poetry for many years.

Libby Falk Jones has published poems in regional and national journals and anthologies and in a chapbook, *Above the Eastern Treetops, Blue* (Finishing Line Press, 2010). Professor Emerita at Berea College, she leads contemplative writing workshops.

Anita Wilkins was born in Wyoming, raised on Montana ranches, went to one-room country schools, eventually Stanford, San Francisco State, traveled, taught, published in anthologies, chapbooks, magazines, is a Pushcart recipient.

Dennis J. Preston is a minister who enjoys reading, writing, traveling, and spending time with his family. *Cloaked Moon: Women of the Bible* is his fourth book of poetry.

Laverne Zabielski, writer, designer, artist, founder and director, The Working Class Kitchen, 1990-1998. MFA

Spalding University, 2004. *The Garden Girls' Letters and Journal*, memoir published by Wind Publications, 2006.

The author of four poetry collections, **Bill Glose** was named the *Daily Press* Poet Laureate in 2011 and featured by NPR on *The Writer's Almanac* in 2017.

Mrs. LaChance has been writing and critiquing poems for the past thirteen years. Favorite subjects are nature and family. She has won several contests along the way.

Margarita Serafimova, shortlisted for Montreal Poetry Prize 2017 and other contests, has work in *Agenda Poetry, London Grip, Waxwing, Trafika, A-Minor, Poetry South, Orbis, Nixes Mate, Minor Literatures, Writing Disorder*, etc.: *https://www.facebook.com/MargaritaISerafimova/*.

Young Smith is an associate professor of English at Eastern Kentucky University, where he is a core faculty member with the Bluegrass Writers Studio, a low-residency MFA program.

Pat Williams Owen went from the left-brain career of legal publishing to the right-brain work of poetry. The shift still sometimes makes her dizzy. Her debut poetry collection, *Crossing the Sky Bridge* was published by Larkspur Press.

ABOUT ACCENTS AND ITS SENIOR EDITOR

Accents Publishing was created in January, 2010 as a poetry press offering handmade poetry chapbooks at an accessible price. We graduated to full-length poetry collections, offered books in translations and various anthologies, added on-demand printing and Ingram distribution, and now we're happy to offer the very first issue of our very first literary journal. We are very proud of the work we've been able to accomplish at Accents. Please take a look at our catalog and support us by buying a book, subscribing to Literary Accents, submitting work to our journal, or telling your friends about us.

Katerina Stoykova is the founder and Senior Editor of Accents. A bilingual author with many interests, she focuses on living life to the fullest and being 100% true to herself.

http://accents-publishing.com/books.html

www.ingramcontent.com/pod-product-compliance
Lightning Source LLC
Chambersburg PA
CBHW020130130526
44591CB00032B/584